Cyber Crimes

CRIME, JUSTICE, AND PUNISHMENT

Cyber Crimes

Gina De Angelis

Austin Sarat, GENERAL EDITOR

CHELSEA HOUSE PUBLISHERS
Philadelphia

Chelsea House Publishers

Editor in Chief Stephen Reginald
Managing Editor James D. Gallagher
Production Manager Pamela Loos
Art Director Sara Davis
Director of Photography Judy L. Hasday

Staff for CYBER CRIMES

Senior Editor John Ziff
Associate Art Director Takeshi Takahashi
Picture Researcher Sandy Jones
Cover Illustrator Takeshi Takahashi

First Printing

1 3 5 7 9 8 6 4 2

The Chelsea House World Wide Web site address is
http://www.chelseahouse.com

Library of Congress Cataloging-in-Publication Data

De Angelis, Gina.
Cyber crimes / Gina De Angelis.
    p. cm. — (Crime, justice, and punishment)
Includes bibliographical references and index.
Summary: Discusses the high tech crimes committed by hackers, crackers, and phone phreaks using computers, including fraud, embezzlement, and espionage, as well as the best ways to minimize the occurrence of such crimes.

ISBN 0-7910-4252-9 (hc)

1. Computer crimes—United States—Juvenile literature.
[1. Computer crimes.] I. Title. II. Series.
HV6773.2.D43 1999
364.16'8—dc21   99-25797
                                                 CIP

Contents

CRIME, JUSTICE, AND PUNISHMENT

CAPITAL PUNISHMENT

CHILDREN, VIOLENCE, AND MURDER

CLASSIC CONS AND SWINDLES

CRIMES AGAINST CHILDREN:
CHILD ABUSE AND NEGLECT

CRIMES AGAINST HUMANITY

CYBER CRIMES

DETERRENCE AND REHABILITATION

DRUGS, CRIME,
AND CRIMINAL JUSTICE

THE DUTY TO RESCUE

ESPIONAGE AND TREASON

THE FBI'S MOST WANTED

FORENSIC SCIENCE

THE GRAND JURY

GREAT PROSECUTIONS

HATE CRIMES

HIGH CRIMES AND MISDEMEANORS

INFAMOUS TRIALS

THE INSANITY DEFENSE

JUDGES AND SENTENCING

THE JURY SYSTEM

JUVENILE CRIME

MAJOR UNSOLVED CRIMES

ORGANIZED CRIME

POLICE AND POLICING

PRISONS

PRIVATE INVESTIGATORS
AND BOUNTY HUNTERS

RACE, CRIME, AND PUNISHMENT

REVENGE AND RETRIBUTION

RIGHTS OF THE ACCUSED

SERIAL MURDER

TERRORISM

VICTIMS AND VICTIMS' RIGHTS

WHITE-COLLAR CRIME

Fears and Fascinations:

An Introduction to
Crime, Justice, and Punishment

By Austin Sarat

We live with crime and images of crime all around us. Crime evokes in most of us a deep aversion, a feeling of profound vulnerability, but it also evokes an equally deep fascination. Today, in major American cities the fear of crime is a major fact of life, some would say a disproportionate response to the realities of crime. Yet the fear of crime is real, palpable in the quickened steps and furtive glances of people walking down darkened streets. At the same time, we eagerly follow crime stories on television and in movies. We watch with a "who done it" curiosity, eager to see the illicit deed done, the investigation undertaken, the miscreant brought to justice and given his just deserts. On the streets the presence of crime is a reminder of our own vulnerability and the precariousness of our taken-for-granted rights and freedoms. On television and in the movies the crime story gives us a chance to probe our own darker motives, to ask "Is there a criminal within?" as well as to feel the collective satisfaction of seeing justice done.

Fear and fascination, these two poles of our engagement with crime, are, of course, only part of the story. Crime is, after all, a major social and legal problem, not just an issue of our individual psychology. Politicians today use our fear of, and fascination with, crime for political advantage. How we respond to crime, as well as to the political uses of the crime issue, tells us a lot about who we are as a people as well as what we value and what we tolerate. Is our response compassionate or severe? Do we seek to understand or to punish, to enact an angry vengeance or to rehabilitate and welcome the criminal back into our midst? The CRIME, JUSTICE, AND PUNISHMENT series is designed to explore these themes, to ask why we are fearful and fascinated, to probe the meanings and motivations of crimes and criminals and of our responses to them, and, finally, to ask what we can learn about ourselves and the society in which we live by examining our responses to crime.

Crime is always a challenge to the prevailing normative order and a test of the values and commitments of law-abiding people. It is sometimes a Raskolnikov-like act of defiance, an assertion of the unwillingness of some to live according to the rules of conduct laid out by organized society. In this sense, crime marks the limits of the law and reminds us of law's all-too-regular failures. Yet sometimes there is more desperation than defiance in criminal acts; sometimes they signal a deep pathology or need in the criminal. To confront crime is thus also to come face-to-face with the reality of social difference, of class privilege and extreme deprivation, of race and racism, of children neglected, abandoned, or abused whose response is to enact on others what they have experienced themselves. And occasionally crime, or what is labeled a criminal act, represents a call for justice, an appeal to a higher moral order against the inadequacies of existing law.

Figuring out the meaning of crime and the motivations of criminals and whether crime arises from defiance, desperation, or the appeal for justice is never an easy task. The motivations and meanings of crime are as varied as are the persons who engage in criminal conduct. They are as mysterious as any of the mysteries of the human soul. Yet the desire to know the secrets of crime and the criminal is a strong one, for in that knowledge may lie one step on the road to protection, if not an assurance of one's own personal safety. Nonetheless, as strong as that desire may be, there is no available technology that can allow us to know the whys of crime with much confidence, let alone a scientific certainty. We can, however, capture something about crime by studying the defiance, desperation, and quest for justice that may be associated with it. Books in the CRIME, JUSTICE, AND PUNISHMENT series will take up that challenge. They tell stories of crime and criminals, some famous, most not, some glamorous and exciting, most mundane and commonplace.

This series will, in addition, take a sober look at American criminal justice, at the procedures through which we investigate crimes and identify criminals, at the institutions in which innocence or guilt is determined. In these procedures and institutions we confront the thrill of the chase as well as the challenge of protecting the rights of those who defy our laws. It is through the efficiency and dedication of law enforcement that we might capture the criminal; it is in the rare instances of their corruption or brutality that we feel perhaps our deepest betrayal. Police, prosecutors, defense lawyers, judges, and jurors administer criminal justice and in their daily actions give substance to the guarantees of the Bill of Rights. What is an adversarial system of justice? How does it work? Why do we have it? Books in the CRIME, JUSTICE, AND PUNISHMENT series will examine the thrill of the chase as we seek to capture the criminal. They will also reveal the drama and majesty of the criminal trial as well as the day-to-day reality of a criminal justice system in which trials are the exception and negotiated pleas of guilty are the rule.

When the trial is over or the plea has been entered, when we have separated the innocent from the guilty, the moment of punishment has arrived. The injunction to punish the guilty, to respond to pain inflicted by inflicting pain, is as old as civilization itself. "An eye for an eye and a tooth for a tooth" is a biblical reminder that punishment must measure pain for pain. But our response to the criminal must be better than and different from the crime itself. The biblical admonition, along with the constitutional prohibition of "cruel and unusual punishment," signals that we seek to punish justly and to be just not only in the determination of who can and should be punished, but in how we punish as well. But neither reminder tells us what to do with the wrongdoer. Do we rape the rapist, or burn the home of the arsonist? Surely justice and decency say no. But, if not, then how can and should we punish? In a world in which punishment is neither identical to the crime nor an automatic response to it, choices must be made and we must make them. Books in the CRIME, JUSTICE, AND PUNISHMENT series will examine those choices and the practices, and politics, of punishment. How do we punish and why do we punish as we do? What can we learn about the rationality and appropriateness of today's responses to crime by examining our past and its responses? What works? Is there, and can there be, a just measure of pain?

CRIME, JUSTICE, AND PUNISHMENT brings together books on some of the great themes of human social life. The books in this series capture our fear and fascination with crime and examine our responses to it. They remind us of the deadly seriousness of these subjects. They bring together themes in law, literature, and popular culture to challenge us to think again, to think anew, about subjects that go to the heart of who we are and how we can and will live together.

*   *   *   *   *

There has never been, nor will there ever be, a society without crime. As society changes, crime changes. As society develops, crime develops. New technologies bring new opportunities for criminality. This is as true in regard to computers as it has been with any other technological advance.

Cyber Crimes brings to this subject a clear-eyed view of the underlying issues in the linkage of crime and computers. It points especially to the need to protect values such as security and privacy that traditionally have been enormously important in American society, and suggests that the computer has had the paradoxical impact of democratizing crime. It takes up in a convincing way the particular dangers associated with pornography and "cyber terrorism." In so doing, this book shows how a new class of criminals is drawn to computer crime and how traditional kinds of crime are adapted to new realities.

It provides a stimulating series of portraits of cyber criminals, all the while raising a series of provocative questions: Are cyber crimes simply old crimes committed using a new technology? Which areas of the criminal law are most important in regard to cyber crimes? Do we need to develop new laws? Are the existing categories of criminality adequate to the new threats? Is cyber crime really just a sub-category of white-collar crime, as is suggested in the conclusion, or is there something entirely new in play?

And, in the end, this book allows us to pose new questions about law enforcement, such as how are computers themselves changing the way we go about enforcing the law and dealing with cyber crimes? It is a fascinating and stark reminder of both the adaptability and ingenuity of crime and criminals.

ARPANET, HACKERS, CRACKERS, AND PHREAKS

The word *cyberspace* was first used in 1982 in science fiction. It is not really a physical location, although we speak as if it is. But the concept of cyberspace is not new; it actually began with Alexander Graham Bell's invention of the telephone in 1876. In fact, the first "cyber crimes" could be said to have been committed in 1878.

Bell's company used many teenaged former telegraph office boys to connect phone calls and to provide information to phone-service subscribers. But soon, as author Bruce Sterling relates in his book *The Hacker Crackdown*, the company encountered problems with its youthful employees:

> The boys were openly rude to customers . . . saucing off, uttering facetious remarks, and generally giving lip. . . . And worst of all, they played clever tricks with the switchboard plugs: disconnecting calls, crossing lines so that customers found themselves talking to strangers, and so forth. This combination of power, technical mastery,

This ad for the movie Hackers *was defaced by real-life hackers on the World Wide Web.*

and effective anonymity seemed to act like catnip on teenage boys.

Bell's company eventually got rid of the boys and began hiring respectable young women, who for the most part did not engage in the same kind of misbehavior.

Just as cyberspace is older than most people think, the idea of the Internet—though many of us have learned about it only in recent years—is older, too. It originated in the early 1960s, when the U.S. military establishment and the RAND Corporation set the goal of using computers to ensure continued communications in the event of a nuclear attack. A system having only one central computer would be too vulnerable to destruction. What we now call "the Internet" was then a loosely linked system of computers that used many, many phone lines to communicate with one another, thereby ensuring that if one route was unable to transmit information, another one would be available.

The networked computers were able to complete tasks and computations much more quickly because their operators did not have to use regular mail to send information in the form of magnetic tapes or punched cards, telling the receiving computer what to do. Instead, the information could be transmitted electronically through telephone wires in an instant.

This Internet prototype originated in 1969 as ARPANET (Advanced Research Projects Agency Network), and it was run by the Department of Defense. For defense purposes, there were many routes, instead of just one, through which the information traveled around the network. ARPANET originally linked the Department of Defense and several universities (the University of California at Los Angeles, Stanford Research Institute, the University of California at Santa Barbara, and the University of Utah). But in 1971, ARPANET was extended to include more universities and government agencies, including Harvard,

Massachusetts Institute of Technology, and the National Aeronautics and Space Administration (NASA).

Then an interesting thing happened. Instead of exchanging computational services, network users began exchanging notes and electronic mail and "talking" to each other on news and discussion groups. And from 1973 on, other countries became connected to ARPANET, as did whole other networks. These other computer networks were compatible with ARPANET because a universal communication language was used: NCP, or Network Control Protocol. (Today this language is usually referred to as Transmission Control Protocol, Internet Protocol, or TCP/IP. You may have noticed that your computer sometimes asks for an "IP Address" when you are surfing the Internet.) At the same time as network protocols were being developed,

Software engineer and programmer Tim Berners-Lee (below) invented the World Wide Web to assist him in his work, and scientists were soon using the Web to monitor research. Criminal users weren't far behind.

domain names were also beginning to be used. For example, instead of trying to find server number 204.50.77.34, you could search for "explora.com" and it would take you to that numerical address.

Unless you knew an employee of IBM or Digital Electronics Corporation, the Internet probably became available to you sometime after 1986, as the affordability and speed of personal computers (PCs) increased. What happened in 1986? That year, the National Science Foundation Network (NSFNET) became the "backbone" of the Internet. The increased speed of its transmissions meant that the Internet could traffic more and more data. According to Explora Multimedia's web page, in 1989 "ARPA stopped managing ARPANET which was integrated into Internet." From Switzerland in 1993 came the World Wide Web, the "net" that many of us now hear about every day.

Linking the world's computers together has resulted in many educational, technological, and financial wonders. Electronic mail, or E-mail, lets us correspond within seconds. "Chat rooms" and "Internet Relay Chats" (IRCs) let us correspond by keyboard with several people simultaneously. And the Internet itself is filled with such a vast array of information that tomorrow's schoolchildren will be unable to complain that "it wasn't in the encyclopedia." But the World Wide Web has also resulted in some wonders of *criminal* behavior.

In February 1995, after a manhunt lasting several years, Kevin Mitnick was arrested and charged with computer fraud. His capture was arguably the most publicized event in the computer world. It has spawned at least three books—one by the person who apprehended Mitnick—and will undoubtedly lead to movies and other retellings. Exactly what did Mitnick do to deserve all this media attention? He gained access illegally to several computer systems, pirated computer programs, and stole long-distance phone services to do it. How could someone so adept at manipulating computer systems and other technologies be caught? Mitnick had been hunted unsuccessfully by federal authorities for two years for his offenses. But over Christmas of 1994, he tried to break into the computer files of Tsutomu Shimomura, a physicist and computer security expert in California. After about six weeks of tracking, Shimomura found Mitnick in North Carolina.

Mitnick had access to thousands of credit card numbers and other important information, and the ability to use that information to steal hundreds of thousands—if not millions—of dollars. But he didn't. He allegedly accessed Department of Defense computers. He had the ability to destroy information or even cause a global military disaster. But he didn't. He gained access to computers holding sensitive information, an action for which he had no authority. Like most computer hackers, Mitnick "looked around" the systems he broke into, then left.

Although many of Mitnick's friends and associates from the late 1970s and early 1980s—the "Roscoe Gang"—allege that he very likely disrupted the phone service of persons he felt had injured or insulted him, these alleged activities are not part of his criminal record. He was given six months' detention and probation at age 17 for stealing electronic manuals from Pacific Bell. And in 1987 Mitnick was sentenced to 36 months' probation for stealing software through a telephone line. At any rate, many writers argue that Kevin Mitnick is not the security threat to every American family that some journalists and authorities have made him out to be. In fact, most hackers are not as menacing as the media implies they are.

Hackers differ from "crackers" in one important way: their activities are generally not malicious. Most hackers are motivated by an intense desire to learn how computer systems work, how to get into them undetected, and how to find their security holes. The thrill of reading information they know they are not meant to see, or of doing something they know is illegal, adds to the pleasure these hobbyists experience. Like any hobby, hacking can be habit-forming. Many hackers spend long hours at their terminals while trying to hold down jobs and have spouses and families. Kevin Mitnick considered divorcing his wife when he felt she interfered with his hacking.

In the 1970s the term *hacker* described a person extremely adept and clever at programming. Later, in the 1980s, it came to mean a person adept at "cracking" new systems undetected. Now, much to the dismay of hackers themselves, the media and authorities like government agencies and police departments use the word to designate anyone accused of a crime involving technology. It is true that hackers who are merely curious can unintentionally cause considerable damage. But the quest for information and learning—not revenge or maliciousness—is what drives most hackers to pursue their hobby so relentlessly.

Crackers, on the other hand, are malicious hackers. They break into systems to vandalize, plant viruses and worms, delete files, or wreak some other kind of havoc. Embezzlement, fraud, or industrial espionage (stealing a corporation's secrets) are just a few of the cracker's possible objectives. Cyber espionage exists between countries as well as between companies, so it poses a danger to our national security. Cyber terrorism is another frightening development, threatening the safety of perhaps millions of people worldwide. There is no disputing that what crackers do is dangerous as well as illegal.

Another form of cyber crime is perpetrated by "phone phreaks." Instead of accessing computer systems, phreaks explore the cyber world through phone lines. Phreaks were among the earliest hackers, operating as early as the 1970s. One incident caused by phreaks, reported in the February 24, 1997, issue of *Computerworld*, involved the New York City Police

Department. Phreaks broke into the NYPD's phone system and changed the taped message that greeted callers. "The new recording said officers were too busy eating doughnuts and drinking coffee to answer the phones. It directed callers to dial 119 in an emergency," wrote reporter Sharon Machlis.

Other hackers and phreaks break into the voice-mail systems of unwary companies that offer toll-free numbers for their customers. They set up their own voice-mail boxes on a company's line. In some cases, they then post the information on the Internet, in effect supplying others with free voice-mail and long-distance phone calls at the company's expense.

Three phreaks in California reprogrammed the telephone lines of three different radio stations to pre-

Commuters exit a New York subway under signs that say "The Hacker Quarterly" and "Volume Fourteen, Number Three" instead of "Watch Your Step" and "Have a Great Day." Computer hackers were responsible for changing the messages.

vent any calls but their own from reaching the stations during on-air contests. The men eventually pleaded guilty to charges of computer fraud. They had won over $20,000 in cash, two Porsches, and two trips to Hawaii for being the "right" callers to the stations.

How great a threat do hackers, crackers, and phone phreaks pose to the rest of us? Which category of cyber criminal is the most dangerous? Against which activities do we most need to protect our systems? Is there any way to completely prevent some hacking into our computer systems and phone lines?

These questions defy simple answers. There is probably no way to prevent all instances of hacking, but we can minimize the occurrence of expensive, potentially disastrous computer crimes. Alertness and good employee management in the form of employee training are arguably the most effective defenses against a breach of computer security.

Many consider Kevin Mitnick a great "social engineer." Countless times, he convinced *sysops* (system operators) and *sysadmins* (system administrators) that he was using their computer systems legitimately. He was also sufficiently pleasant and convincing on the phone or in person with secretaries or security guards to get passwords and other important information from many companies, which he would then use to break into their computer files.

Another instance of "social engineering" occurred in 1976, when Jerry Schneider performed an embezzlement of several thousand dollars live on the popular television show *60 Minutes*. Schneider called the "right" people, gave a bank clerk the account number of host Dan Rather, and then said into the phone, "ten thousand dollars." "You can't simply call on the telephone and get one's credit extended from $500 to $10,000!" exclaimed an incredulous Rather. Schneider responded, "Yeah you can." He had in fact done it, on network television.

But computers themselves are merely tools. *People* commit computer crimes, and other people as well as computer files can serve as sources of protected or sensitive information. The good news, however, is that people can also prevent computer crimes. The more we all learn about different kinds of computer crime, and the tools that are being developed to stop it, the more secure we will all be.

The
Information
Age

Our society's most valuable commodity is not grain, steel, or even technology; it is information. Because of computer networks, just about everyone can now access an astounding range of information. There are no borders in cyberspace. The Internet is international—even though 80 percent of Internet use occurs in the United States—and a staggering amount of information on every subject imaginable is available for free.

Because so many people now have access, computer crimes have become democratized. Just as every American citizen who wants to can run for elected office, everyone with a computer and modem can commit a computer crime if so inclined. Anyone, conceivably, could become a "white-collar" computer criminal.

When the term *white-collar crime* came into wide use several decades ago, it was thought that certain crimes were committed by persons whom no one would normally suspect of criminal behavior: professionals,

Computer networks now link the world at the touch of a finger— erasing international boundaries.

23

"white-collar" (as opposed to unskilled or semiskilled "blue-collar") workers. White-collar crimes were typically committed by professionals because they were the ones with the ability—and the access—to commit crimes like embezzlement, imposture, and forgery. Certainly, blue-collar workers could commit these crimes as well. But Edwin Sutherland, a criminologist, coined the term *white-collar criminal* to help make other scholars aware that not all criminals fit the stereotypical image—that is, not all came from the lower socioeconomic classes. In the late 1990s, however, the term *white collar* is somewhat inaccurate: the playing field has been leveled by the widespread use of computers. Now "white-collar crime" tends to mean simply "nonviolent crime" or "economic crime."

As technology becomes increasingly accessible to more and more people, it also becomes a potential tool for increasing numbers of criminals. Most computer crimes do not involve violence but rather play on greed, pride, or some other character weakness of the victim. They are based on dishonesty, not force. For these reasons computer crimes are considered white collar. There is no legal definition of the term *white-collar crime*, but there is a working one: most white-collar crimes are committed without the use of force, and therefore require a higher degree of planning than, for example, armed robbery. Some sociologists believe the people who commit these crimes are distinguishable from "street" or "common" criminals—or at least, that they once were distinguishable. One police officer who specializes in computer crime remarks that "the average guy we arrest has got a bachelor's degree. They plot and plan." And today's computer crime, he continues, "takes a lot more skill" than the "attention-getting stunts" that were often pulled by computer hackers in the early 1980s.

Just as the term *white-collar crime* designates several very different kinds of crime, so the term *computer crime* is similarly broad. It encompasses crimes that are committed with a computer, crimes that occur in cyberspace, and crimes committed against a computer. Some of these crimes are completely new, while others are older crimes that merely use the computer as a tool. The endless and constantly growing variety of computer crimes makes it difficult to pass laws that adequately cover new computer crimes. Some crimes, such as embezzlement, wire fraud, and forgery, are already covered under existing law. Others, such as cyber vandalism, cyber terrorism, and cyber espionage, are relatively new. For these newer crimes, the letter of the existing law sometimes does not allow prosecution of what is clearly criminal behavior.

As millions of people all over the world gain access to high technology, computer crimes can be committed by almost anyone with the will and the wits to break the law—or even just the ambition to learn everything possible about computer systems and software. Nearly all white-collar crimes now involve the use of computers or telecommunications, according to Vic Sussman of *U.S. News and World Report*. This is more likely the result of our dependence on computers, rather than any technological skill on the part of most "regular" criminals. But "regular" or "street" criminals are also becoming increasingly adept at crimes involving technology such as pagers and phone systems, as well as computers.

The business world of stock trading and high finance is an obvious example of an industry dependent on computers to keep records and transfer huge amounts of money across many miles, though many other important industries and services are "techno-dependent" as well. As more and more computers become connected to one another and as all of us begin to operate in an increasingly "cashless" society—relying on credit, debit, and ATM cards instead—computer crimes will surely increase. Law enforcement organizations and computer and software corporations will race to keep ahead of

The floor of the New York Stock Exchange. Billions of dollars change hands electronically every day on the world's financial markets, presenting a huge potential target for cyber criminals.

cyber criminals by creating and enforcing new computer security measures.

Who are these cyber criminals? Although the stereotypical cyber criminal is a young, male, "geeky" loner type with too much free time and a penchant for breaking into networks, the reality is somewhat different. The typical computer criminal is actually someone else.

Just as most white-collar crimes are committed by employees and ex-employees of the victimized company, 75 to 80 percent of prosecuted computer crimes are committed by current or former employees. "We must go beyond the stereotypes in talking about who commits the wide range of computer crimes," says author and cyber crime expert Buck BloomBecker. Despite all the media attention they have been given, hackers account for a very small percentage of computer crimes. As one reporter notes, "Hackers have learned to commit crimes, and criminals have learned to hack."

There are many different kinds of computer crimes, ranging from identity theft to sexual harassment to otherwise ordinary white-collar crimes that just happen to involve a computer. The most common form is online theft and fraud. Phreaks, crackers, and sometimes hackers illegally access and use voice-mail, E-mail, and network access accounts—which constitutes toll fraud or wire fraud. Reporter Sharon Machlis quotes Walt Manning, a former police officer who now works as a security consultant in Texas, as saying, "We had a client who lost $4.5 million over a three-day period" from this kind of computer break-in. One company found out that it had been victimized only after a woman called to ask about its free voice-mail services!

Long-distance access codes are in great demand by hackers, crackers, phone phreaks, and street criminals alike. Vic Sussman writes, "One university discovered this the hard way when its monthly phone bill, a staggering $200,000, arrived in a box instead of an envelope." Some cyber criminals obtain the codes by "shoulder-surfing"—looking over the shoulders of unwary people in phone booths. One reason this is a common form of crime among hackers and phreaks is because they tend to run up enormous phone bills pursuing their hobbies for 10 to 12 hours a day. Others obtain the codes from "pirate" electronic bulletin boards, where they are posted in exchange for free software, credit card numbers, or other information.

Hackers, crackers, and phreaks are nearly always interested in obtaining free phone usage. In Russia, for example, authorities have discovered that many hackers are willing to assist cyber cops and other officials in exchange for free Internet access time. The Internet is in great demand, yet few Russians have the resources to pay the equivalent of $3 an hour for access. The authorities there, as well as officials from large Internet access companies like America Online, hope that giving hackers free access in exchange for information—an ironic bargain—will help secure the Internet and other computer networks from any serious security breaches.

Software piracy is another growing and seemingly insurmountable problem. It is illegal under American copyright laws, but most software piracy actually takes place overseas. And federal copyright laws are often insufficient even to prosecute U.S. citizens, as illustrated by the famous case of David LaMacchia. LaMacchia, a student at Massachusetts Institute of Technology (MIT), distributed free software through a bulletin board service (BBS) on MIT computers. After a Federal Bureau of Investigation (FBI) probe, LaMacchia was indicted in 1994 for conspiracy to commit wire fraud. The software he offered reportedly had a total value of over one million dollars, but LaMacchia argued that he had not distributed the software for financial gain and therefore could not have violated the federal copyright laws. The case was dismissed.

Internationally, it is estimated that software piracy costs American companies up to $5 billion a year. One book, *Approaching Zero*, notes that many countries are known as "single-disk" nations—"countries where one legitimate copy of a software program is bought and the rest are illegally copied." The book lists Taiwan, Thailand, Hong Kong, Singapore, Brazil, India, and Japan as markets where software piracy is rampant. Software piracy is also common in China and has become an issue in U.S. diplomatic and economic relations with that country.

A billboard advertising Microsoft's Windows 95, Beijing. Rampant software piracy in China and several other nations costs U.S. companies an estimated $5 billion annually.

In a case of domestic software piracy, a student at the University of Puget Sound was found to be distributing over 100 free software programs from a personal web page on the university's network. "Some of the software packages retailed for more than $3,700 apiece," says one reporter. The student's web page was shut down, the university reprimanded him, and the Software Publishers Association went after a more stringent penalty. But ultimately, the student was made to write a 20-page paper on copyright infringement at universities and to perform 50 hours of community service. "Many in the computing world were surprised when the Association went after the Puget Sound student and then settled for the equivalent of a rap on the knuckles," author Karla Haworth wrote in the July 11, 1997, *Chronicle of Higher Education*. The difficulty in prosecuting many cases of software piracy, even in the United States, is evidenced by both the LaMacchia and the Puget Sound cases. But software piracy is also, in addition to being tough to prosecute, an extremely common form of computer crime.

One of the most frightening cyber crimes is identity theft. This kind of fraud is much easier than it once was, because a wealth of personal information is available online for free, and even more personal information is available for a small fee. Did you know that if your family's name is in the phone book, your family's address and telephone number are probably available on the World Wide Web—and it doesn't matter whether or not you have a computer!

You might wonder how all this personal information got onto networked computers in the first place. You will recall that the first networked computers were government computers. As computers became more and more affordable and easier to use, private companies began to use them to keep records, just as the government had been doing. Computers became, in the words of journalist Peter McGrath, "repositories for the most intimate details of people's lives. Anyone who opened a bank account was leaving electronic traces of his or her house payments, buying habits, visits to the doctor. Telephone service created trails leading to families and friends. Even a social-security number was a potential liability: with it, a dedicated sleuth could pry the holder's tax returns loose from government computers."

Now that driver's license numbers are also stored on computers, which are usually part of a larger network, a person's physical characteristics—eye color, height, and so on—are also available. Magnetic strips on credit cards and ATM cards require computers to read them and to keep records of the millions of transactions made every day.

Now that faster and faster computers are becoming more available and more affordable, this kind of personal, confidential information is becoming more readily available to those with the time and energy to pursue it. As McGrath points out, "computers themselves operate at speeds that were unthinkable a few years ago: personal computers running Intel's Pentium chip are more than 300 times faster than machines with the same company's first-generation chip, the 8086."

Fortunately for all of us, not everyone with access to or interest in this kind of personal information will take advantage of it in a criminal way. But many will. Writing for *Newsweek* in July 1997, reporter T. Trent Gegax covered the case of Kathryn Rambo, a victim of identity theft. Someone found Rambo's personal information from an employee benefits form, dropped it into Internet databases and search engines, and then applied for credit using that information. The impersonator "had a new $22,000 Jeep, five credit cards, an apartment and a $3,000 loan," all using Kathryn Rambo's personal information and good credit record.

Charles Pappas, author of a column called "Safety Net," reported on the case of Beverly Reed. Ms. Reed's purse was stolen in 1991; a few months later she discovered that her identity had been stolen as well. The thief was also named Beverly Reed, but she was using the first Ms. Reed's Social Security number to establish a line of credit for herself. Beverly Reed #2 had defaulted on $36,000 in loans, ruining Beverly Reed #1's credit rating and preventing her from refinancing her house.

Pappas conducted his own investigation to find out just how much personal information is available on the Internet. He looked up an old friend and found that some information was available for free. Much, much more was available for very small sums. Pappas wrote, "It took me about two days and $50 to find out more about him than his spouse probably knows. This was just the tip of the information pyramid. With a bigger budget, I could easily have obtained my friend's driving history, criminal record, workers compensation claims, and more."

Pappas notes, however, that identity theft did not suddenly emerge because more people have begun to surf the Internet; identity theft also occurs when criminals go through people's garbage to find receipts and other sensitive information. But he quotes Angie Farleigh of the California Public Interest Research Group, who believes that the recent increase in the number of identity theft cases is indeed computer related: "Our database has exploded with the number of new cases—we now have over 5,000. . . . There's no way to tabulate it, but I'm convinced the Net is making identity theft so much easier."

Like identity theft, some other cyber crimes are not new, except that perpetrators now use computers to commit them. For example, money laundering—making illegally acquired or "dirty" money look legal or "clean"—has been committed for many decades. But a money launderer using computers is able to carry out the crime much more quickly and efficiently, just as computers enable legitimate workers to do their jobs more quickly and efficiently. The *Economist* reported in July 1997 that programmers are actively developing new computer systems that would make money launderers' crimes much easier—and even harder for law enforcement to detect: "There are stored-value cards, which allow customers to load money onto a microchip-bearing piece of plastic. This can then be carried around like a credit card. There are computer-based systems, for example, those involving payments over the Internet. And there is talk of hybrid systems, which allow smart cards and network-based payments

U.S. Attorney Donald Stern discusses the arrest of a teenager in Massachusetts who broke into an airport's communication system.

to work together." (Smart cards are cards that work like cash; at the time of this writing they were still in the prototype stage and had not been released for use by the general public.)

In some types of cyber crimes, like "cyber laundering," the use of a computer makes the crime harder to detect or to prove. "Salami slicing" is a crime that uses computers to make electronic transfers of funds from hundreds or even thousands of separate accounts.

The dependence of the banking industry on computers, along with the trend toward an increasingly cashless society, has opened up opportunities for technically savvy thieves.

Because the stolen amounts are small, most account holders don't notice the theft. But small amounts add up, of course, and the thief can end up rolling in stolen money.

Insurance fraud (lying to an insurance company in order to collect policy money), investment schemes, and work-at-home schemes are all present in cyberspace, just as they are in real life. One journalist writes that it is possible for "cyber pirates" to "register phantom ships on the computers of maritime agencies," then take out insurance policies on the ships and "wreck" them. Although insurance fraud has probably existed as long as insurance itself has been around, the use of computers to commit and then cover up the crime is indeed new.

Sometimes the line between computer crimes and "regular" crimes is blurry. In Michigan, for example, there were three separate cases of fraud involving a subway ticket machine. The judge ruled that taking advantage of the machine's security loopholes did not constitute computer crime, because the machine was nothing more than a glorified soda machine. In other words, the crime was against a vending machine, not a computer.

The enormous range of computer crimes means that all of us should be concerned about computer security, regardless of our individual level of computer expertise. World financial systems rely heavily on computers, as do national defenses, private businesses, and, increasingly, personal correspondence. "The average American should be concerned," says Ray Kelly, Undersecretary for Enforcement at the Treasury Department, "because virtually every aspect of their daily lives is now involved in infrastructure and, increasingly, the cyber infrastructure—information."

"We are all usees," in the words of Buck BloomBecker, whether or not we actually use computers, because we all rely on them. We must not view computer crime as an exotic activity. To do so would prevent us from seeing that it endangers each one of us.

CYBER TERRORISM: THE CRIME OF THE FUTURE?

Walter Laqueur, an expert on terrorism at the Center for Strategic and International Studies, points out that one U.S. intelligence official "has boasted that, with $1 billion and 20 capable hackers, he could shut down America." Laqueur notes that while terrorists traditionally target political leaders for assassination, take hostages, or stage random attacks on public or government facilities, the damage that can be done by electronically attacking computer networks would be "far more dramatic and [produce] lasting results." This cyber terrorism, Laqueur believes, would be much more devastating to huge numbers of people than would biological or chemical warfare, for example.

But how dangerous are hackers, really? Could a

A scene from the movie WarGames, in which a teenage hacker nearly causes a global nuclear war. The vulnerability of military computer networks to casual hackers—or worse, to terrorists—concerns many experts.

37

teenager cause World War III, as the one played by Matthew Broderick in the 1983 film *WarGames* nearly did? Or is cyber terrorism just a phantasm, a terrible nightmare dreamed up by super-paranoid people?

Many government and military officials warn that just because a major incident of cyber terrorism has not yet occurred, there is no reason for complacency. Journalists David Freedman and Charles Mann offer the following chilling projections:

> The U.S. Department of Defense has more than 2.1 million computers linked to some 10,000 local networks, which are tied to 100 long-distance networks. These networks, the Pentagon says, are under siege.
>
> According to data from the Defense Information Systems Agency, the military may have experienced a quarter of a million attacks in 1995, the most recent year for which figures are available. More than likely, DISA believes, about two thirds of the attempted intrusions were successful; typically, fewer than one percent were detected. Many attacks on these military systems are trivial pranks, like the pornographic defacing of the Air Force's main Web page last December [1996]. But some are not. . . . If, as DISA suggests, the number of incidents is doubling every year, the Department of Defense networks will be attacked a million times in 1997. Computer crime is a major threat to national security.

Cyber terrorists, like "regular" terrorists, have a political motivation for their crimes. However, the risk is not limited to government computers; the systems of private corporations and even nonprofit groups are also vulnerable. Almost any computer contains information cyber terrorists might want, depending on their particular political goals. Government computers, however, are often the target of cyber spies as well as terrorists.

One famous incident of cyber espionage that could have had disastrous consequences is outlined in Cliff Stoll's 1989 book, *The Cuckoo's Egg*. In 1986 Stoll, then an unemployed astrophysicist, was hired as a system administrator for Lawrence Berkeley Laboratory in California. He found a 75¢ accounting error and then, tracking the error, discovered that a hacker had been accessing the laboratory's files. After alerting federal authorities, he tracked the hacker and found a group of West German teenagers breaking into American military network computers. The hackers, members of the Chaos Computer Club based in Hannover, were selling American military information to the KGB, the intelligence agency of the Soviet Union.

Stoll's book brought the Chaos Computer Club, already famous in Germany, to the attention of many Americans. Despite its name, and the fact that several of the club's teenage members were actively involved in selling secrets to international intelligence agencies, the Chaos Club was for the most part simply a group of eccentrics intensely interested in computers and network capabilities. In other words, according to some authors at least, it was far from a vast terrorist conspiracy.

But is cyber terrorism a real possibility? In 1991, during the Gulf War, which pitted Iraq against a coalition of nations led by the United States, an 18-year-old Israeli was charged with breaking into Pentagon computers. The young man apparently read secret information on the Patriot missile, a key American weapon used to defend against attacks by Iraq's Scud missiles. In another incident during the same war, teenagers in the Netherlands broke into U.S. military computers—army, navy and air force—at 34 different sites. "Once inside the computers," writes Karen Judson, "the intruders read crucial data on military personnel, the type and amount of military equipment being moved to the gulf, missile targeting, and the development of important weapons systems. Evidence also indicated that the hackers were looking for information about nuclear weapons." Another article claims that the teenagers were actually crackers who didn't just read the files, but "stole information about troop movements

Neal Patrick, a young computer hacker, testifies before the U.S. House of Representatives, September 26, 1983. Patrick had broken into computers at the Los Alamos National Laboratory, a nuclear research center.

and missile capabilities . . . and offered it to the Iraqis." The intrusions occurred on several occasions between April 1990 and May 1991, according to a U.S. official.

What exactly could malicious hackers, American or foreign, do to endanger the average American? In October 1997, more than 125,000 people in San Francisco were without power because of what may have been an act of sabotage. If crackers with evil intentions break into the computers of power companies, water companies, emergency services, telecommunications systems, banks, or any vital industries—and we already know that some crackers have that capability—entire communities could be thrown into chaos.

"The airline control system, passenger reservations, air traffic control; all of those are controlled by information networks," said Buck Revell of the Institute for the Study of Terrorism and Political Violence in a 1997 interview with CNN. "These networks extend on a global basis. And they can be interceded and intercepted."

What can we do to protect ourselves from such threats? The U.S. government has formed the Infrastructure Protection Task Force, or IPTF, to investigate the possibility of electronic terrorist attacks on vital industries and services. The IPTF includes members from several government agencies, such as the FBI; the Central Intelligence Agency; the National Security Agency; the National Communications System; and the Departments of Defense, Energy, Justice, Commerce, Transportation, and Treasury.

According to the FBI's homepage (fbi.gov), there are eight infrastructures that require attention and protection:

- telecommunications (such as the phone company and networked computers)
- electrical systems (power companies)
- gas and oil production, storage, and transportation
- banking and finance
- transportation (such as airlines, railroads, and highways)
- water supply systems
- emergency services (ambulances, police, firefighters and other rescue personnel)
- government services.

The IPTF classifies possible threats to these infrastructures as either physical threats—bombing, for example—or cyber threats. Cyber threats are numerous and varied: a terrorist attack could take the form of "electronic, radio-frequency, or computer-based attacks on the information or communications components that control critical infrastructures."

In October 1997, a group of malicious hackers may have broken into classified files in the Pentagon computer network. The group, known as "Masters of Down-

SONOMA, NAPA, MARIN, N. CALIF. - Microsoft Internet Explorer

File Edit View Go Favorites Help

Address   Links

The Hacked NetDex.Inc

netdex
internet
inc.

Complete Internet Services

This Page Has Been Hacked By Analyzer
I hacked this page in order to make things right
Makaveli did NOT hacked any of those DOD systems
he dont even know how to trojan a system
if u searching anyone u should search for me.

Hackers like to brag about their abilities—sometimes enhancing their reputations by exaggerating their expertise, sometimes telling the frightening truth.

loading/2016216," used an Internet site to brag about its achievement in April 1998. Reporter John Vranesevich interviewed (via an Internet Relay Chat) two members of the group, which consists of Americans, Russians, and Britons. Although neither the Pentagon nor the Defense Information Systems Agency would confirm the break-in, the hackers claimed that they would release or sell the classified files they downloaded. Vranesevich noted that this incident differs from others because "what we're seeing here is a group of mostly adults . . . who sat down and planned . . . and strategically went after a system with the sole goal of gathering files." Such a break-in is, of course, much more threatening than the simple "cyber graffiti" or other pranks undertaken by most hackers. To make matters worse, the alleged crackers did not believe they ran a real risk of being captured.

Some of this bravado may just be typical hacker behavior. If hackers don't brag about what they've done or can do, they won't cultivate any online reputation—which is a ticket to more information. But if most hackers' bragging contains even a kernel of truth, then cyber terrorism and cyber espionage are not simply frightening fantasies, but real possibilities.

Computer viruses and other "cyber critters" are one means that terrorists or malicious hackers could use to shut down important computer systems. Viruses, or "self-replicating programs," are programs written for the express purpose of infecting other systems, usually through a diskette but sometimes through Internet or electronic mail networks. Viruses carry a "payload," which is designed to change or even attack the system they enter. Some viruses may be able to attack system files and "melt" a computer's motherboard, erasing all data from the hard disk and making the computer a useless pile of parts. Most viruses, however, amount to harmless pranks.

The first documented computer virus was "Brain," developed by two young men in Pakistan in 1987. Brain was probably the first international computer virus, although it was not intended to cause damage. But a month later, another virus surfaced at Lehigh University in Pennsylvania, and this one was intentionally damaging.

Other cyber critters include *spiders* (search engines) and electromagnetic pulses that can "melt" a computer's hard disk. *Trojan horses* are viruses that slip in along with an ostensibly helpful or useful program, and then release dangerous code. *Rabbits* "order a computer to perform useless tasks endlessly, multiplying ever more work orders until they finally overwhelm the computer and it can cope with nothing else," according to authors Paul Mungo and Bryan Clough. *Worms* can access a system but can't spread outside the network through, for example, a diskette. Worms take up residence in a computer and use up space until the machine slows down or crash- es. (Robert Morris's experimental "Internet worm" of 1988 was surprisingly—if accidentally—effective: it shut down over 6,000 computers.)

Logic bombs are "always deliberately damaging, but unlike viruses, don't replicate. They are designed to lay dormant within a computer for a period of time, then explode at some preprogrammed date or event. Their targets vary: some delete or modify files, some zap the hard disk; some even release a virus or a worm when they explode," according to Mungo and Clough. Logic bombs are favorites among disgruntled ex-employees, because they can set the "bomb" to go off at any point after their departure from a company. In 1985, a former employee of Minnesota Tipboard Company, angry at being fired, demanded payments each week he was unemployed. If he wasn't paid, he threatened to set off a logic bomb that would erase important data from his former employer's computers. This person's plan was thwarted when the company hired a computer security expert who defused the bomb.

At least one famous virus has a "logic bomb" built into it. On March 6, 1992, about 10,000 computers worldwide would not start up. A virus called Michelan- gelo was the culprit. Michelangelo's payload was pro- grammed to be released on the birthday of the famous artist (hence the virus' name). The Michelangelo virus was first discovered in April 1991. Some people, having heard the warnings beforehand, avoided the problem by not booting up their computers on the following March 6. Still, several large organizations were affected, including the New York City subway system and Drex- el Burnham Lambert, a brokerage firm. Computers in Britain, Japan, and South Africa were also hit.

Michelangelo infected the section of a diskette that starts up—the boot sector. Once inside a computer, it attached itself to the master boot records (the part of the hard disk that starts the computer). When an infected computer's calendar told it that March 6 had arrived (even if this internal calendar was wrong), the boot sector of the computer's hard disk was overwritten and any data stored there was destroyed. In most cases, the computer would not boot up again, and the overwritten data could not be restored. Michelangelo is still dormant in some computers, awaiting March 6 of each year. Now, however, all antivirus software can detect Michelangelo before any damage is done, and program "vaccines" can fix the problem.

Paul Mungo and Bryan Clough, the authors of *Approaching Zero: The Extraordinary World of Hackers, Phreakers, Virus Writers, and Keyboard Criminals*, say that viruses were never as common as the media would have us believe. They cite as an example of user hysteria the so-called Cookie Monster virus of the 1970s. The Cookie Monster, a character from the popular children's TV show *Sesame Street*, would supposedly appear and ask for a cookie. When the user typed the word *cookie*, it would go away. If the user did not type the word, the Cookie Monster would become more insistent and prevent any further work from being done. But the Cookie Monster was actually not a virus, say these authors. It was just a prank, and unlike a true computer virus, it couldn't replicate itself.

Computer viruses and other "cyber critters" definitely pose a continuing threat. Any piece of programming that can shut down computers—in a world where many necessary services are run by computer—is a serious danger.

Technological capability combined with political instability can create an especially explosive mix. Many computer viruses come from eastern European countries and from Russia. Internationally, thousands of viruses are probably propagating at any given moment. Bulgaria, in particular, became a "virus factory" in the late 1980s. Some of the cleverest and most damaging viruses in the world were written by "Dark Avenger," a

Viruses can wreak havoc with computer systems—doing anything from making the text wobbly and unreadable (as above) to completely shutting down an entire system.

young Bulgarian. Since writing viruses is not a criminal offense in Bulgaria, even if it were possible to trace the virus writers, they would not face any legal penalty.

Communism, both in the former U.S.S.R. and in Bulgaria, "produced skilled mathematicians and terrible computers" in the 1980s, according to journalist Christian Caryl. It also spawned many young computer programmers who were quite talented at finding ways around technological obstacles. Political and economic instability in these countries means that talented computer professionals are tempted to sell their skills to the highest bidder—even if that bidder is an international terrorist group.

The possibility of political cyber crimes increases as more and more people become more skilled at computer programming and at hacking into computer systems. But cyber terrorism and cyber espionage are not the only criminal threats to computer networks. Cyber criminals can, and do, violate the privacy and security of individuals, rather than entire nations.

Welcome to the Hottest Internet link for the Wildest Unc Adult Pleasures!

Warning! You must be 18 years of age (21 in some areas) or older to visit the WWW sites and services listed contain adult, XXX material not suitable for minors. Viewing these sites if you are under age is prohibited by and is subject to prosecution by the applicable authorities. By clicking below you agree to being familiar with being 18 (21 in some areas) or older and that the viewing of adult material is legal in your area. Furthermore this type of material offensive and you release and discharge all involved in the production and maintenance of liabilities.

Click to continue

send mail to xxx@adultsex.com

If you do not agree with the above, are under age or concerned about sex on the Internet cli

sored Erotic

ese sites and services
eral, state and local laws
laws of your community,
agree that you do not find
s site from any and all

below.

CYBERSEX: THE CRIME OF THE PRESENT?

This chapter examines a different kind of computer crime: intensely personal violations that often have to do with sex or gender. Cyberspace has been called a "virtual" world in part because the people who dwell there and the behaviors that take place there parallel those of the real world. So it follows that the kind of crimes taking place in the real world would also happen in cyberspace. Stalking, sexual harassment, rape, and child abduction are all crimes that will continue to befall people in the real world regardless of whether or not we continue to rely on computers in our society. But just as many criminals increasingly use computers to commit white-collar, "victimless" crimes, a growing number use computers to seek out individual victims for harassment and intimidation.

The Internet is littered with sites containing graphic sexual images. But the online world harbors other, less obvious, dangers for children—and adults.

There are at least two documented cases of police officers who saw attractive women and then tracked them down through computer searches. One of the officers repeatedly pulled a woman over, not because she had committed a traffic violation but to ask her for a date. The other officer also harassed his targets, whose addresses and phone numbers he obtained by searching computerized police databases of license plate numbers. These two men could still have committed their crimes without the help of computers, but the added ability of computers to conduct rapid, thorough searches made it easier for them to find potential victims.

Another potential danger is pornography in cyberspace. The threat is threefold. First, children may be able to access hard-core pornography on the Internet.

John Grabenstetter (left) was sentenced to seven years in prison in Buffalo, New York, for trafficking in child pornography over the Internet.

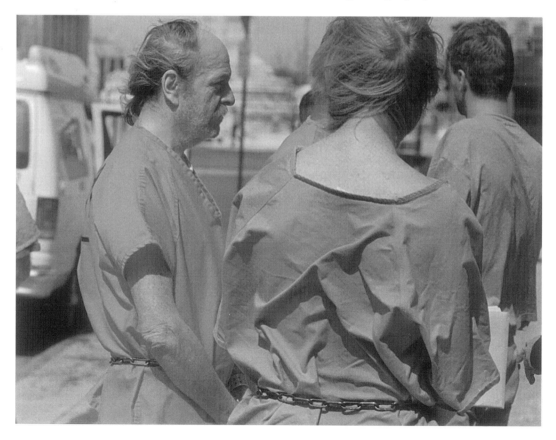

Although several companies market products to help parents keep kids away from objectionable sites, parents still need to monitor their kids' explorations through cyberspace, just as they would monitor any of their children's other activities.

Second, child pornographers have found an easy way to sell their materials—thereby perpetuating the sexual abuse of children. The transmission of adult pornographic photos and the online sale of pornographic videos and similar materials is not illegal nationwide but may violate local obscenity laws. In 1995, Robert and Carleen Thomas, who ran an electronic bulletin board system (BBS) that was not open to the general public from their home in Milpitas, California, were convicted of federal obscenity charges. They were also charged with violating local laws in Memphis, Tennessee, when a postal inspector used the Thomases' BBS to download graphic images involving bestiality and sexual fetishes. Their pornographic materials, though illegal in Memphis, could easily be downloaded in defiance of the local laws. This case was very controversial because adult pornography is legal in most places. What if, for example, the police officer who downloaded those pictures had been living in Denmark? Could a case against the Thomases then have been constructed? Furthermore, not everyone who wandered onto the BBS could download the images; interested persons had to fill out an application and pay $99 a year.

On the other hand, child pornography—graphic materials depicting or suggesting sexual acts involving anyone under 18 years of age—is illegal throughout the United States. Creating such materials is abusive toward the children involved and exposes the perpetrators to a number of separate criminal charges.

Child pornography does exist on the Internet. In 1995, the FBI arrested 12 pedophiles (adults who are sexually attracted to children) whom they had been monitoring through America Online, a large nation-wide online service. One of the men arrested ran a day care center. There was no evidence to suggest that any children from the day care center were photographed for the suspect's child pornography, but the crime is chilling nonetheless.

In another case a year later, a 19-year-old college student was arrested and charged with promoting a sexual performance by a child. He used his Internet account at Adelphi University "to retrieve, from computers in Sweden and the Netherlands," child-porn photos, which he would then send to people in the United States.

The third—and biggest—threat to children online is that pedophiles and other dangerous persons will lure their victims to real-life encounters through chat-mail or E-mail correspondence. Online, you can fake your whole identity. You can become anyone you want to be, you can lie about your age, your gender, and other characteristics that make you who you really are. This anonymity makes people feel free to express themselves fully. But it also facilitates the luring of victims.

In 1992, two police officers conducted a cyber sting operation. Mark Forston, a 49-year-old man, was a BBS operator who distributed child pornography through electronic correspondence. Forston thought he had befriended a 15-year-old boy with the online name "Look," whom he arranged to meet in real life. Forston planned to take pornographic photos of "Look" (which he would then distribute or sell) and had rented a motel room for sexual relations with the boy. But "Look" was actually an undercover police officer. After Forston's arrest, a young man named Bryan Cox came forward. Cox claimed that Forston had lured him in much the same way two years earlier and had molested him.

In March 1994, a young man in Massachusetts was charged with using a BBS to enlist the help of a teenager in kidnapping a child for sex. This kind of abduction

Children must learn that dangerous people can be met over the Internet as well as on the streets of towns and cities. John D. Rex (shown here) raped two boys he met on the computer. Rex was sentenced to 20 to 25 years in prison for the crimes.

is nothing new, but computers and E-mail have added another dimension. Bulletin board systems and other new methods of communication have "become the new playgrounds," says one police officer. Just as pedophiles have traditionally targeted playgrounds and other places where children congregate, so the Internet is one big "playground" where many children can be found and approached.

The danger online is admittedly not as great as some fearmongers would have us believe. Journalist Kevin Whitelaw claims that "over 35 million Americans use the Net, and the number of incidents remains small." Author Mark Stuart Gill further maintains, "The most sensational [computer] crimes," including those involving pornography, "are a small percentage of Internet crimes." It is difficult to find precise statistics, however, because the number of Internet users is constantly increasing, and many crimes are hard to detect. Also, most of the available statistics on computer crime involve software piracy and theft, toll fraud, and wire fraud. Cases of child abduction or abuse that began on the Internet are relatively few.

Nevertheless, it is imperative that youngsters understand that cyberspace contains some dangerous people, just as the real world does. But in cyberspace, dangerous individuals can easily disguise themselves. Kids need to learn certain rules about cyberspace. For example, they should never give out personal information (such as home address or phone number), just as they shouldn't give such information out to a stranger in person. (Other suggestions are available in the pamphlet "Child Safety on the Internet Highway," from the Interactive Services Association and the National Center for Missing and Exploited Children, 1-800-843-5678.)

Children aren't the only ones at risk. In 1996, the body of a Maryland woman was found in a shallow grave behind the home of a North Carolina man she had met on the Internet. The man claimed that she had asked him to torture and kill her. Another young woman filed charges in New York against a man she had met online, claiming that he had held her captive and sexually assaulted her. In both cases, the victims had allegedly written sexually stimulating messages over the Internet to the accused men. Cyberspace may not be a land of fantasy where people can express themselves without fear, after all. If cyberspace is in fact just as dangerous as the rest of the world, then people must learn to be on their guard as much as they would in any other context.

Harassment and stalking happen online too. Robert Maynard and his wife, Teresa, were victims of a cyber stalker in 1996. The Maynards helped found Internet America, an online services provider in Dallas, Texas. When harassing and insulting messages about the Maynards appeared on BBSs and did not stop, Robert Maynard went to court. Interestingly, the judge in the case served the restraining order over the Internet, sending an E-mail to the alleged harasser. Fortunately for the Maynards, the harassment did not spill over into a physical attack.

But what if cyber harassment *does* spill over? One woman who mentioned in a chat room that she was a lesbian was harassed online. But she was also eventually beaten by two men who entered her home. She sustained injuries requiring more than 60 stitches and plastic surgery. She notes, "I live in fear because I am still the subject on some [chat groups]." One of the men who attacked her was never captured.

In another incident, a writer named Jayne Hitchcock was harassed through a form of imposture. Woodside Literary Agency, with whom Hitchcock had had some unpleasant dealings, posted fake messages on the Internet. These messages, supposedly from Hitchcock herself, were designed to cause her harm or at the very least severe distress. One of the fake notes read:

> Female International Author, no limits to imagination and fantasies, prefers group masochistic/sadistic interaction, including lovebites and indiscriminate scratches. . . . Contact me at misc.writing or stop by my house at [actual home address]. Will take your calls day or night at [actual home phone number]. I promise you everything you've ever dreamt about. Serious responses only.

Hitchcock filed a $10 million lawsuit after she

received nearly 30 phone calls from interested people who had read that message. What if any of them had actually shown up at Hitchcock's home?

The messages were apparently posted in retaliation. Hitchcock had posted messages of her own to a writers' group on the Internet, warning about the business practices of Woodside. Someone at the agency then began a campaign to discredit Hitchcock professionally: insulting E-mails, also supposedly from Hitchcock herself, were sent to colleagues at a college where she taught part-time. And Hitchcock's literary agent received E-mails saying that their professional relationship should be terminated. Fortunately for Hitchcock, her name was misspelled in the fake E-mail, tipping her agent off to its false origins. This kind of online harassment and stalking ruin the personal and professional reputations of victims—in addition to threatening their safety.

Laws against stalking, in both the real and virtual worlds, allow for protection of the victim. This means that even though the suspect may not have actually harmed the victim, he or she can still be arrested. Just the intention to harm—if it can be shown to be a serious one—is enough to get a stalker arrested. In online stalking cases, however, it is possible that judges will lean toward the accused rather than the victim, since cyber stalking by nature involves less of a physical threat to a victim than does real-life stalking.

The Jake Baker case raised some important questions about privacy and fantasizing online, as well as about what law enforcement can do to prevent violent crimes in the face of evidence that they may occur. Baker, a student at the University of Michigan in 1994–95, wrote fiction. He wrote short stories about sexual torture and rape. He posted his stories on an appropriately labeled area of the Internet—the alt.sex newsgroup—with warnings to readers that the stories were graphic and explicit. One story in particular, featuring a female victim who was an actual member of one of Baker's classes at the university, caught the eye of an alumnus. University authorities were notified.

Baker also corresponded by E-mail with a person named "Arthur Gonda," and the two shared their sexual fantasies, which included abducting and raping young women. In one often-quoted E-mail, Baker said, "Just thinking about it anymore doesn't do the trick. I need TO DO IT." The E-mails described several young women in Ann Arbor, Michigan, and in Baker's hometown, who might make suitable victims for the two men.

Baker was arrested in February 1995 and became the first person ever to be charged with transmitting interstate threats via the Internet. Baker himself insisted that he never meant to hurt anyone, and never planned to. He maintained that his stories were just that—stories. The charges stemming from the stories were dropped, but the charges of interstate threats held. After much controversy, the case against Baker was dismissed in January 1997 when a judge ruled that the E-mails, since they were private and intended only for "Arthur Gonda," did not constitute a real threat of immediate harm.

Some observers believe that the Baker case represents a kind of "thought crime." Law enforcement, they claim, moved against the student for what he believed, not for what he did, and that is completely alien to the American criminal justice system. Another example of an alleged thought crime is the 1994 case of a 51-year-old man who was arrested in California by a computer-crimes detective. The man was carrying a vibrator, sexual lubricant, and condoms in his car—in expectation of meeting a 13-year-old boy he had befriended on a BBS and lured into a real-life encounter. At the time of his arrest, he had committed no real crime, but this was only because the 13-year-old he was expecting to meet did not exist.

Guaranteeing the First Amendment rights of online pornographers while protecting children from inappropriate material is a perplexing problem. This page: One aspect of the problem graphically demonstrated. Opposite page: A possible solution—software that blocks access to certain Internet sites.

Some people believe that police overstep their boundaries when they pose as children and wait for propositions. These people believe that the power to arrest a person before he or she commits a crime is too great a power to give government, and that it violates individual rights. Others argue that such undercover operations, when conducted lawfully, protect those children (or adults) who would otherwise be victims.

Often in the past, authorities had no power to protect the victims of stalkers until actual harm was committed by the stalker. But for too many victims, the first incidence of physical harm proved fatal. It is for this reason that laws protecting victims of harassment and stalking are now more stringent, and authorities have more leeway to prevent violence from occurring in the first place.

Whatever lawmakers' intentions, however, they must still protect individual rights in accordance with the Constitution. New modes of communication, like BBSs and E-mail, only emphasize the need to balance individual rights with the rights of a whole community of others.

The First Amendment to the U.S. Constitution guarantees American citizens freedom of speech, freedom of religion, and freedom of the press. However, some kinds of speech, such as slander (false oral statements that defame an individual) and libel (published material that is false and defamatory), can result in a lawsuit; and incendiary speech (inciting a mob to commit murder, for example) can result in a criminal prosecution. But most speech—even so-called hate speech, which might express contempt for a particular racial group, for example—is protected by the First Amendment. The answer to ugly words, according to the spirit of this amendment, is not censorship, but more words.

The First Amendment, as with many parts of the Constitution, can be interpreted in various ways. Its creators could have had no idea of how their document would need to adapt to the future. They purposely ensured its flexibility, yet stated clearly that the freedoms outlined in the First Amendment were not conditional.

Although the First Amendment protects the free-speech rights of pornographers, laws have been passed to restrict access by minors to adult materials. However, the Internet is a completely new mode of communication. Some materials, such as child pornography, that are legal in other countries but illegal in the United States are available worldwide 24 hours a day on the Internet. Congress, as well as several state governments, has enacted "decency" laws in the interest of protecting children from some materials on the Internet (such as homemade bomb formulas). Opponents of decency laws argue that it is not the government's responsibility to protect children, and that people have a right to disseminate all types of information.

Several bills have been introduced in an attempt to regulate materials on the Internet. The most famous of these is the Communications Decency Act (CDA). Congress passed the CDA in 1995, immediately creating a First Amendment furor. Supporters of the law argued that the act would protect children and other innocent parties from being exposed to harmful materials. It would force businesses and Net-citizens to "keep it clean." Opponents countered that any attempt to regulate or even define indecency on the Internet would violate the First Amendment right to free speech. For 48 hours after the bill was signed into law, thousands of websites voluntarily went black in protest. The Supreme Court decided the case, *ACLU v. Reno*, in June 1997, ruling that the CDA was unconstitutional and could not legally be enforced. Several federal courts have also found unconstitutional, state laws seeking to regulate online content.

On November 20, 1998, the Supreme Court halted enforcement of another indecency law until its constitutionality could be resolved in court. This law is the Child Online Protection Act, or COPA (sometimes called CDA II), which was passed as part of the Omnibus Appropriations Act, a mammoth piece of legislation determining, among other things, the federal budget. The law, supporters say, addresses some of the problems in the original CDA and will protect children. Again, opponents claim that any law restricting online content is unconstitutional. The Electronic Frontier Foundation, the Electronic Privacy Information Center (EPIC), and the American Civil Liberties Union (ACLU) filed suit to stop enforcement of the law and won a temporary restraining order. These organizations work for freedom of speech online and believe that any laws restricting free speech are not only unconstitutional but also set dangerous precedents for the relatively new medium of cyberspace.

Legal debates will continue for as long as we have a First Amendment, and for as long as Americans remain concerned about their right to free speech. The Internet is a form of communication that in some respects resembles older forms, such as newspapers, books, and magazines. In other ways, however, it is entirely new. Similarly, cyber laws bear some resemblance to older legislation, but in some ways they are entirely new. A balance must be reached between the rights of individuals to have free access to information, and the rights of the entire population to enjoy a safe online environment.

CYBER COPS

Are computer criminals really light-years ahead of law enforcement? Or is the playing field just about level, since cops also have access to computers? Quoting Carlton Fitzpatrick, a computer crime expert at FLETC (Federal Law Enforcement Training Center), in Glynco, Georgia, author Bruce Sterling writes, "Cops in the future will have to enforce the law 'with their heads, not their holsters.' Today you can make good cases without ever leaving your office. In the future, cops who resist the computer revolution will never get far beyond walking a beat."

Police officers building cases without leaving their offices may sound far-fetched, but that's precisely what police lieutenant Bill Baker did. Baker, who works in Kentucky, successfully broke a child-pornography ring operating in the United Kingdom. According to journalist Vic Sussman, "an E-mailed tip from a source in Switzerland led Baker to an Internet site in Birmingham, England. After about three months of investigation that involved downloading 60 pages of file names related to child porn and 400 images, Baker called on Interpol, New Scotland Yard and police in Birmingham, who arrested the distributor." So it seems that authorities certainly can match hackers in computer literacy.

Some police officers have been specializing in computer crimes since the 1970s. But Keith Lowry, a "cyber cop," maintains that using high-tech gadgets and technical knowledge to solve a cyber crime is not always necessary. Once, when Lowry was trying to figure out a confiscated hard drive's password using a software program designed to crack codes, he found a slip of paper attached to the back of the computer. It was the password—apparently written down so that the criminal wouldn't forget it.

Another time, Lowry was given a pager that a thief had dropped while robbing a jewelry store. He "electronically manipulated" the pager and got its serial number. Still, Lowry says, "The truth is, a lot of high-tech police work is just old-fashioned street smarts." If he was unable to retrieve the pager's serial number electronically, for example, Lowry could have called the pager's manufacturer or service provider and asked if anyone had canceled service or reported a pager missing in the last 24 hours.

Computer crimes can occur anywhere, and they are often virtually untraceable. Most local police departments lack the skilled personnel or the funds to combat computer crime, especially since cases can involve several jurisdictions at once. Who, then, is responsible for fighting cyber crime?

The U.S. Secret Service is best known for protecting the president and the First Family. But the Secret Service originated in 1865 as a Treasury Department police force that combated counterfeiters. It still performs that role, and by order of Congress, the Secret

Service fights computer crime as well. Title 18 of the U.S. Code (U.S.C. Section 1029) gives the Secret Service jurisdiction over "access device fraud." An access device is defined as "any card, plate, code, account number, or other means of account access that can be used, alone or in conjunction with another access device, to obtain money, goods, services, or any other thing of value, or that can be used to initiate a transfer of funds."

Title 18 doesn't mention computer crime specifically, but this section of the U.S. Code makes the Secret Service responsible for tracking hackers who use stolen long-distance codes, who sell credit card numbers, or who give passwords to other hackers to help them break into systems. There is a limitation on which cases the Secret Service can take on, however. "First, the offense must 'affect interstate or foreign commerce' in order to become a matter of federal jurisdiction," author Bruce Sterling explains. This is not a very strict limitation, as nearly everything that happens on large computer networks crosses state lines. "The second limitation," Sterling continues, "is money. . . . Federal crimes must be serious; Section 1029 specifies a minimum loss of one thousand dollars." In other words, not every computer crime merits the attention of the Secret Service.

According to the next section of Title 18, Section 1030 (d), the Secret Service will carry out its duties under the authority of the secretary of the Treasury and the U.S. attorney general. The attorney general also happens to be the head of the FBI. This means that there is naturally some overlap between the two agencies.

The FBI has a special force, the National Computer Crime Squad (NCCS), which is responsible for investigating violations of the Federal Computer Fraud and Abuse Act of 1986. This act addresses computer break-ins that cross state or international lines, that involve intruding into federal or state computers, or that involve accessing financial or medical records. The NCCS also investigates any break-ins of telephone company or other major computer networks, industrial espionage, bank fraud, organized crime, and software piracy. Pirated software and stolen computer components, including chips and laptops, are estimated by one writer to cause annual losses of over $24 billion worldwide. According to the FBI's NCCS web page, it also investigates "other crimes where the computer is a major factor."

Other government organizations also fight computer crime. The Infrastructure Protection Task Force (IPTF), discussed in Chapter 3, is responsible for coordinating government and private efforts to protect our nation's critical infrastructures. Although this entails guarding against more than just computer crimes, computer security is undoubtedly a major concern of the IPTF. Many of the infrastructures that the IPTF oversees are already operated primarily by computers, and the protection of these industries is crucial to American life.

In addition to the IPTF, there is the U.S. Air Force Office of Special Investigations (OSI), which, according to Bruce Sterling, is the "only federal entity dedicated full time to computer security." Another highly effective government agency is the Federal Computer Investigations Committee (FCIC), unofficially formed in 1986, when it was known only as "the Colloquy." Sterling calls the FCIC "the most important and influential organization in the realm of American computer crime." Among all the cyber-crime-fighting groups, Sterling credits the FCIC as "the first to really network nationally and on a federal level."

But the FCIC is not your average government agency. It has no real office. Its mail is delivered to the Fraud Division of the Secret Service, but the committee itself consists of computer security experts from all imaginable places and areas of expertise: telephone company employees, local and state cops, private investigators, Secret Service officers, FBI agents, lawyers, programmers, military personnel, and IRS agents. Its members do not work full time for the FCIC, but rather collaborate with one another on particular cases when necessary. They go back to their "primary" jobs when they're no longer needed.

How can such an unorthodox organization operate efficiently? Sterling notes that most computer-crime-fighting organizations are forced to work this way by the very nature of computer crime. The FCIC simply cannot afford to get bogged down in details such as publishing handbooks or regulating itself, as other government agencies must. The speed of emerging technological advances—and of communications in cyberspace—prohibits this. Therefore, as Sterling noted in 1990, "The FCIC is the trainer of the rest of law enforcement. . . . If the FCIC went over a cliff on a bus, the U.S. law enforcement community would be rendered deaf, dumb and blind in the world of computer crime." The methods used by the FCIC seem to foreshadow the way cyber cops will have to be organized in the future.

Other, nongovernmental organizations include the International Association of Computer Investigation Specialists, or IACIS, and the Computer Emergency Response Team (CERT), which will be discussed in Chapter 6. Thanks to the FCIC, FLETC, CERT, and similar organizations, even local police departments that do not have a special "cyber crime force" become more aware of computer crime. The number of police officers and detectives who are familiar with computers and with the tested methods of tracking cyber criminals is increasing daily.

In addition to so-called cyber cops, there are private citizens who help prevent computer crime and track down perpetrators. Tsutomu Shimomura, the physicist who tracked Kevin Mitnick, is only one of many pro-

Private citizens have formed groups to help police the Internet. The hacker shown above works for a group called Ethical Hackers Against Pedophilia.

fessionals with the ability and willingness to trace hackers, crackers, and phone phreaks who have crossed the line between innocent exploration and malicious damage.

One need not be a computer professional to be a successful cyber tracker. Even amateur computer users are sometimes able to track hackers. Robert Morris's famous "Internet worm" of 1988 was tracked and contained within 24 hours by volunteer "computer geeks" across the country. Jeff Schiller, Ted Ts'o, Stan Zanarotti, Bill Sommerfeld, and Jon Rochlis were among the team of computer users who worked through the night of Wednesday, November 3, to isolate the Internet worm and "reverse engineer" the damage that the worm's coding had done.

In a similar but less well known case related in the March 1997 *Chronicle of Higher Education*, two college students traced a hacker and notified authorities within about three hours. The hacker had vandalized the website of the National Collegiate Athletic Association (NCAA). The two students, Jay Kamm at Duke University in North Carolina, and Benjamin DeLong at the University of Massachusetts, did not know each other but worked together via electronic mail to track the hacker through clues in the "cyber graffiti" phrases he scribbled on the website. The clues led to the address of a computer owned by a 14-year-old boy. DeLong and Kamm wrote a four-page report and gave it to the NCAA the next morning.

Investigations of computer crimes by amateurs are not, of course, the norm, and this case involved simple vandalism. What about computer crimes in which the perpetrators make off with valuable data? Cliff Stoll's book *The Cuckoo's Egg* chronicled the successful tracking and capture of a potentially dangerous espionage ring. Again, this is hardly a routine occurrence. Interestingly, hackers who have given up their illegal hobby or who have been caught and agree to cooperate often make excellent trackers.

At least one author encourages young people interested in hacking to consider a career in law enforcement or computer security instead. Bruce Sterling notes that officials are rapidly gaining ground on computer crime:

> Feds can trump hackers at almost every single thing hackers do, including gathering intelligence, undercover disguise, trashing, phone-tapping, building dossiers, networking, and infiltrating computer systems—criminal computer systems. Secret Service agents know more about phreaking, coding, and carding than most phreaks can find out in years, and when it comes to viruses, break-ins, software bombs, and Trojan horses, feds have direct access to red-hot confidential information that is only vague rumor in the underground.

The desire for praise and esteem from other hackers, a driving force behind many break-ins, can also be satisfied by joining forces with the "good guys." Writes Sterling, "There are few people in the world who can be so chillingly impressive as a well-trained, well-armed U.S. Secret Service agent."

Still, controversy continues over the methods of computer crime enforcement officials. How far should police be allowed to go in pursuing and prosecuting computer criminals, particularly hackers? What about the electronic privacy of average citizens? How should individual rights be balanced with the authorities' need to investigate and build cases?

Sometimes software and other tools are caught up in the debate. Encryption software—programs that transform text into an unreadable jumble of letters and

Robert Morris, seen below leaving court with his mother, was the author of a famous computer virus in November 1988 that was tracked down with the assistance of a team of volunteer "computer geeks."

numbers—is a powerful way for consumers of computer technology to ensure their privacy and the security of their communications. But powerful encryption software was at one point considered a munition by the federal government. It was originally developed, like the forerunner of the Internet, for use by the U.S. military forces and is considered vital for the protection of national security. At first, federal government and law enforcement officials backed the use of the "Clipper chip," which would permit citizens to use strong encryption to protect their computer files while at the same time giving the government a decryption "key." The key was to be used only when encrypted files might contain evidence relevant to a criminal investigation or a national security matter, and only after law enforcement officers had demonstrated "probable cause" and had obtained a court order. (These are the same rules that apply when law enforcement officers want to initiate a wiretap.) However, government officials gave up on the Clipper chip when they realized that American software manufacturers would not produce it and few consumers would be willing to purchase it.

Like encryption, anonymous re-mailers protect the privacy of criminals as well as honest people. Re-mailers are E-mail forwarding sites that "resend" electronic mail from pseudonymous addresses, making it untraceable. Such technology can be beneficial, protecting people who contact authorities to report crimes, or people who speak out against corruption. But police officers and others worry that tools such as encryption and anonymous re-mailers will also give "criminals, terrorists, child abductors, perverts and bombers . . . an environment free from law enforcement or a search warrant," as one FBI agent has put it.

Others claim that encryption and re-mailers are essential to protecting the average citizen's privacy. Should law enforcement agents have the right to break

Equipment and software seized in the course of a computer crimes investigation. Critics charge that law enforcement often casts too wide a net in confiscating computer hardware and files, trampling citizens' Fourth Amendment rights and sometimes crippling legitimate businesses.

into people's files while investigating cases of cyber crime? How can they build a case without access?

Laws about computer crimes have historically been vague. But how can computer criminals be charged when there are few laws defining their alleged crimes? Rich Bernes, an FBI agent in California, asks, "Suppose someone accesses your computer and downloads files. What should she be charged with? Burglary or trespassing? Wire fraud or copyright violation?"

Again, because of the speed of technological advances and the increasing number of computer crime cases over the last few years, the laws are already less fluid now than when this agent made the above comments in early 1997. Still, building a case against computer criminals without infringing on individual rights is often a daunting task.

In some cases, it is claimed, "the feds" have gone way overboard. Often cited as an example is 1990's Operation Sundevil, a large-scale crackdown on hackers. Critics charge that in carrying out this operation, the FBI and other law enforcement agents routinely overstated "probable cause" in seeking to obtain court permission to seize and search computers. This practice, the critics argue, amounted to a violation of the Fourth Amendment's prohibition of unreasonable searches and seizures. According to them, what happened to Steve Jackson Games, Inc.—perhaps the most important Operation Sundevil case—is a perfect example.

Steve Jackson Games (SJG) was a company that published books and other materials about live role-playing games. Dungeons and Dragons is an example of this kind of fantasy game. These are not computer games; they are games played with paper and pencil, dice, and other gaming pieces. Steve Jackson Games also ran a BBS known as "Illuminati," which was frequented by a loyal following of customers and other gamers.

When authorities arrested a hacker named "Urvile," among the documents they found in his home were numerous role-playing materials from SJG. Urvile, apparently, was interested in role-playing games as well as in computers. A friend of his, "Mentor," was not only involved in Urvile's hacker club, the Legion of Doom, but was also employed at SJG. So the Chicago Task Force and the Secret Service raided SJG's offices and confiscated its computers and other equipment.

U.S. Attorney General Janet Reno meets with justice and interior ministers from around the world to discuss combating the use of computer technology by international criminals.

Bruce Sterling describes what happened:

> Jackson's company lost three computers, several hard disks, hundreds of floppy disks, two monitors, three modems, a laser printer, various power cords, cable cords, and adapters. . . . The seizure of Illuminati BBS deprived SJG of all the programs, text files, and private e-mail on the board. The loss of two other SJG computers was a severe blow as well, because it caused the loss of electronically stored contracts, financial projections, address directories, mailing lists, personnel files, business correspondence, and, not least, the drafts of forthcoming games and gaming books. No one at Steve Jackson was arrested. No one was accused of any crime. No charges were filed. Everything appropriated was kept as "evidence" of crimes never specified.

Law enforcement officials believed that SJG computers contained hacker manuals, instructions for committing computer crime, and other unlawful materials. They believed that they had found the computers where several arrested hackers were getting or storing stolen information. But neither Steve Jackson nor any of his employees were ever charged with a crime, and while the authorities held SJG's computers, the business was crippled. In 1993, SJG was awarded damages and attorneys' fees by a federal court, which called the raid careless, unjustified, and illegal.

After the raid on SJG, the Electronic Frontier Foundation was formed. John Barlow, Mitch Kapor, and John Gilmore founded this group to protect the constitutional rights of the "residents" of the digital underground. (EFF can be contacted at 1001 G Street, N.W., Suite 950 East, Washington, DC 20001, or at the EFF website, http://www.eff.org/.)

Operation Sundevil showed the American public that law enforcement was cracking down on computer crime. Still, the case raised important issues that have long been debated in the United States. Since the birth of the nation, Americans have struggled to maintain a balance between individual freedoms and the security of society. Finding that balance in the cyber world may be particularly tricky.

6.

"INFOJUSTICE": WHAT DO WE DO WITH CYBER CRIMINALS?

As long as there are computers, there will be computer criminals. But what can we do about it? Are hackers and crackers the biggest threat? Do hackers even realize their actions are criminal? How should computer criminals be punished? And, finally, how can we protect ourselves from them?

Buck BloomBecker, director of the National Center for Computer Crime Data in Santa Cruz, California, is the author of *Spectacular Computer Crimes*. In his book, BloomBecker presents eight basic types of attitudes that hackers exhibit toward computer systems. "The Playpen" describes the outlook of many hackers—that cyberspace is a toy. Some authors of computer viruses may also have this attitude, but they take their games to a more damaging extreme than do hackers.

"The Land of Opportunity" is the attitude of employees who, perhaps inadvertently, learn about loopholes in security while on the job. They commit computer crimes mainly because the opportunity pre-

Computer hackers "Mudge" and "Weld Pond" testify before the U.S. Senate about lax computer security.

sents itself; they do not decide to commit a crime and then look for a way to do it.

"The Cookie Jar" describes the way some computer criminals with expensive habits—drugs, gambling, playing the stock market—see the cyber world. These persons feel their financial problems are "unshareable," and so they simply dip into "the cookie jar" to pay off their debts.

In "the War Zone" scenario, the criminal is angry, malicious, and hostile. Most viruses are authored by War Zone types, one of whom is probably Bulgaria's "Dark Avenger." Another example of War Zone behavior is the disgruntled or fired employee who vengefully sabotages the employer's computer system. Donald Burleson, angry with his former employer, planted a worm in the company's computer system that, according to BloomBecker, "was capable of destroying 168,000 records of employee commissions." Fortunately for the other employees, the company had backups and was able to minimize the damage Burleson caused.

"The Soapbox" describes the mentality of a computer criminal who wants to make a political statement. Logic bombs, malicious damage, and cyber terrorism are manifestations of this attitude. The Chaos Club, the notorious group of German hackers, is one example of a group of "Soapbox" cyber criminals. (Although its individual members may have felt differently, the club as a whole was aligned with Germany's Green Party, a leftist group opposed to nuclear weapons.)

"The Fairyland" is how many people who are largely ignorant of computers may conceptualize cyberspace. These people are not always aware they are doing anything wrong or destructive. "If people who love computing," says BloomBecker, referring to those of the "Playpen" attitude, "could teach those who live in a fairyland, security might be dramatically increased."

If cyberspace is a "Toolbox" to a computer criminal,

it is simply a means to an end—that is, the computer is a tool in an otherwise ordinary crime. BloomBecker uses the examples of people involved in gambling, prostitution, drugs, and other illegal activities—like organized crime rings—who use computers to keep track of their businesses.

Finally, there is "Cyberpunk Space," which involves new levels of maliciousness. "Cyberpunks" share an apocalyptic vision of the technological future (think of the 1982 movie *Blade Runner*, and you have probably envisioned the world that many Cyberpunks inhabit in their minds).

"Mudge," a former computer hacker, now is hired by Fortune 500 companies to find weak spots in their systems.

Phone phreak Joe Engressia could imitate the phone company's multifrequency tones, enabling him to place free long-distance calls. Like many hackers, Engressia wanted to use his network expertise in a paying job. Most companies balk at hiring former hackers, however.

Whatever their "type," what should law enforcement do with computer criminals? How harshly should they be punished? These are important and difficult questions.

Did Kevin Mitnick, for example, deserve a sentence of seven years in prison? He was held without bail and allowed only monitored phone calls while incarcerated and awaiting trial. Usually this type of treatment is reserved for violent criminals who pose a clear threat to the physical safety of others. Some writers think that the acts Mitnick committed—while they should not be condoned—did not merit such stringent measures. These writers believe that Mitnick merely used a tool that many of us are unfamiliar and uncomfortable with, which raised fears about what the Kevin Mitnicks of the world could potentially do to the rest of us. One journalist believes that hackers like Mitnick do us all a service—by making us aware of holes in computer security.

Others advocate that hackers be hired, not hounded. "We don't know what to do with computer criminals once they've done their time," says Buck BloomBecker. "After the media has lionized them, real competitive life returns these criminals to problems which may well have preceded their computer crime." How can American society allow these criminals to work with computers again? On the other hand, how can we keep them away when they are obviously skilled and driven workers?

Many hackers do indeed make excellent computer security professionals and programmers—in an industry that is growing exponentially and always needs skilled personnel. A "good" hacker like Michael Synergy would surely be in demand. During the 1980s Synergy broke into a credit agency and found financial information on 80 million Americans, including President Ronald Reagan. He also found a group of approximately 700 people who shared the same credit card and all had bizarre credit histories, as if they had simply appeared out of nowhere. Synergy realized he was looking at the names and addresses of people in the federal Witness Protection Program, which gives witnesses against such criminals as organized crime leaders and drug kingpins new identities and addresses to protect them from retaliation. Synergy contacted the FBI and told them about the hole in the system. But not every hacker would have done so, leaving those files vulnerable to future break-ins.

Other hackers and phreaks want (or once wanted) very much to work for the companies they victimized. Joe Engressia, a legendary phone phreak, was famous for being able to mimic Bell Telephone's multifrequency tones by whistling, enabling him to make free calls. Engressia was quoted as saying, "I want to work for Ma Bell. . . . There's something beautiful about the system when you know it intimately the way I do." Far from hiring him, however, the phone company chose to monitor his phone use and refused to provide home service. Even Kevin Mitnick appears to have desired a job working with computers—within "the establishment" that he seemed to hate. In fact, Mitnick reportedly does work with computers now at a health services firm in California.

But many firms are unwilling to hire a hacker who has "done time"—or who has simply been investigated but not charged or convicted. This leaves former hackers with little or no way to make a legal living with computers, despite their great technological skill and their interest in and facility with security and systems management—and despite the huge, industry-wide need for such skills.

Other writers point out that hackers—or crackers, more precisely—use their skills to victimize others, so they shouldn't be rewarded. There exists the potential for real economic and technological damage if we place our trust in onetime cyber criminals, these writers claim. They believe that hackers like Kevin Mitnick must be prosecuted as an example to would-be hackers everywhere. Computer crimes spur endless debate about what is just treatment of suspects, what constitutes a just sentence for those convicted, and whether the actions of hackers are serious crimes even if they cause no tangible loss.

In response to a writer who said that Internet worm

author Robert Morris should not be punished for simply running an experiment that went awry, one sysop
(systems operator) remarked, "You didn't have to clean
up the mess he made." The time employees spend
"cleaning up" the messes intruders make, and the
income lost during "downtime," when the company's
computers are disconnected from networks to be fixed,
could easily run into the millions. Even if the loss fig-
ures are inflated by companies in order to get the attention of federal enforcement agents, as some writers and
hackers claim, the costs to small or midsized companies
might still be in the hundreds of thousands.

Computer criminals, like all white-collar criminals,
present a problem in terms of justice. How should they
be sentenced? Harshly, because of the amount of economic damage they can do? More harshly than violent
criminals? Or leniently, because physical force was not
involved? How can victims of cyber crime be compen-
sated? An additional problem presented by computer
criminals is how few of them have actually been prosecuted and sentenced. There exists little case law and
few sentencing guidelines for prosecutors and judges to
follow. How have some hackers and crackers been punished in the past?

Pat Riddle, a young man from an affluent Philadelphia family, downloaded files from ARPANET and sold
them between 1979 and 1981. He also ran a huge scam,
creating a fake corporation and stealing several hun-
dred thousand dollars' worth of computer equipment, as
well as free electric and phone service for people in his
neighborhood. Riddle was arrested in July 1981 but got
off fairly easy—partly because in 1981 few people were
familiar enough with computers and phone phreaking
to bring the case to trial. Riddle claims a lawyer told
him that he would not be convicted, because no jury
would be able to understand what he did. Riddle was
indicted on standard fraud charges because there were
no computer crime laws yet. He was able to plea-bar-

gain so that he received just a $1,000 fine and two years' "phone probation."

Compare Pat Riddle's case with that of Nick Whiteley, who in 1990 did time in a British prison for hacking into a university computer system and just looking around. (Although Whiteley was British, several countries take their cues from how the United States treats computer criminals because the overwhelming majority of computer users are in the United States.) The difference in severity of the two men's respective crimes, relative to the severity of their punishments, reflects the great shift in public attitudes toward hacking, a shift that took place between 1980 and 1990. One factor in this shift is that more and more people became familiar with computers and what they could do. Another is that more and more businesses, schools, and government agencies began to use computers, making people more concerned about hacking. After Kevin Mitnick's treatment (he was ultimately sentenced to two years in prison), the hacker community also became increasingly nervous.

Leslie Lynne Doucette's sentence was the most severe ever given to a female hacker—a rare breed, according to authorities. Still, the 27-month prison term Doucette received as the result of a plea bargain seems mild by comparison with what she could have received if convicted on all 17 counts she faced of violating federal computer and fraud laws: an 89-year prison sentence and more than $1.6 million in fines and restitution. Between January 1988 and May 1989, Doucette had run a ring that traded access codes, using at least 152 contacts all over the United States.

Craig Niedorf, also known as Knight Lightning, was a coeditor of the electronic newsletter *Phrack*, a legend in the hacker underground. Niedorf had published in his newsletter portions of a document known as "E911," which had been taken from BellSouth during a computer break-in. Niedorf himself, however, had nothing to do with the break-in; that was the work of his associate, Robert Riggs (known as "Prophet"), a codefendant in this case. The charges against Niedorf were finally dropped in July 1990, but he was stuck with thousands of dollars in court costs and legal fees.

Niedorf's was a bad situation, but it could have

A member of the Chaos Computer Club talks about infiltrating top-secret space research computers.

turned out much worse. "Prophet" and two other hackers, "Urvile" and "Leftist"—who, like "Prophet," were members of a hacker club known as the Legion of Doom—were sentenced to prison. "Urvile" and "Leftist," both first-time offenders, plea-bargained and were given 14 months; "Prophet" had pleaded guilty to a charge of conspiracy—his second offense—and was sentenced to 21 months. The crackdown on *Phrack* and "the Atlanta Three," as the hackers came to be called, was part of Operation Sundevil.

Markus Hess, Peter Carl, and Dirk-Otto Brzezinski ("Dob"), all members of the Chaos Computer Club, were indicted for espionage. At their trials in January 1990, it was discovered that the damage they did was actually lighter than had originally been assumed. The three received sentences ranging from 14 months to two years and fines of up to several thousand dollars. Nevertheless, all three were ultimately put on probation in lieu of their prison time. Meanwhile, a fourth suspect, Robert Anton Wilson, died under mysterious circumstances before authorities could arrest him. Hans Hübner, known as "Pengo," was also involved, but he bargained for immunity in return for telling authorities all he knew about Chaos's illegal activities. But Karl Koch (also known as Hagbard Celine) paid the ultimate price. A member of Chaos and one of the first to sell stolen information, Koch was found burned to death in the woods outside Hannover. His death was ruled a suicide, but many believe it was murder.

♣   ♣   ♣

New legislation is being written to address computer crime issues that are not covered under existing laws. And, as we saw in Chapter 5, law enforcement is keeping up with technologically advanced criminals. Legislators and law enforcement officials struggle almost daily to balance the rights of the individual with the

REPORT CHILD PORNOGRAPHY!

Congressman Nick Lampson of Texas at a press conference announcing a bill designed to curtail the use of the Internet by child pornographers and molesters.

protection of the larger community. As police officers become more adept at tracking computer criminals, new products such as software and databases are being developed to make law enforcement's job easier. At the same time, as more cyber crimes are detected and more criminals punished, case law is created and precedents are set for dealing with similar instances in the future. Computer advocacy groups and "watchdog" organizations like WELL and the ACLU keep an eye on law enforcement, while law enforcement keeps its eye on illegitimate activities involving computers. In this way, a healthy balance between individual rights and community security is possible. Because of this cyber crimes might decrease in the future, even as our reliance upon computers continues to increase.

Still, the best prevention of most crimes—computer or otherwise—lies in greater awareness. If more people become aware of the current forms and methods of computer crime, then fewer people will be victimized. The hundreds of computer security consulting firms springing up across the nation and the world offer additional protection as they shore up weaknesses in computer systems and software.

Although encryption is a good way to protect the privacy of E-mail correspondence, one writer notes that concentrating on high-tech gadgetry and complex electronic computer security can have drawbacks. In an article aptly titled "Lock the Damned Door!" writer Robert Scheier exposes security risks in an unnamed southwestern hospital. He notes that while the hospital director was very careful about preventing hackers from breaking into the computer system from outside the hospital, the building's actual physical security was quite lax.

For example, the consultants hired to find weaknesses in security were unable to access the computer's medical files, "but who needs passwords when there's a pile of patient files and X-rays sitting on a nearby desk?" asks Scheier. The consultants, who had no special passes or uniforms, were never stopped or questioned by hospital employees, who were unaware that there was a security review going on. And the metal detector installed in the doorway to the emergency room was a good idea, but only if the back door to the E.R.—which had no metal detector—was locked. Paying attention to high-tech crime prevention cannot replace old-fashioned common sense in preventing crimes of every type.

If the unthinkable does happen and you are hit with a computer break-in, your best bet is to contact the

Computer Emergency Response Team (CERT) at www.cert.org. This organization was founded in 1988 by the Software Engineering Institute at Carnegie Mellon University in Pittsburgh. Working chiefly with Internet users to prevent computer crimes, CERT also knows what to do after crimes have been committed, or in the face of full-blown emergencies. The group, which also keeps statistics on computer break-ins and security threats, reported that threats to the Internet increased from 132 in 1989 to 252 in 1990, and by 1992 the number was a whopping 773. (Remember, the Internet is only one network among hundreds in the world!)

Information about computer security is available not only from CERT, but also at www.ovnet.com/~dckinder/frmain01.htm as well as at many other sites available through a standard web search.

S. M. Lieu writes in "Netsurfer Focus" at www.net-surf.com/nsf/v02/02/index.html that there are many ways to protect your computer system from being infiltrated. The key is to look for possible security breaches that you may not have thought of previously. For example, there are three components to every computer system: the software and hardware, the people, and the procedures. Securing a system means inspecting all three components for possible security breaches. Is there an untrustworthy employee (or boss)? Vulnerable software? Weak passwords? Do people have access to files they don't really need to see? These factors can all lead to computer crime.

Likewise, every computer system faces three basic threats: acts of malice, acts of ignorance, and acts of God or nature. To completely secure a system, it's important to remember that other potential dangers besides hackers, crackers, and phreaks exist.

If your computer is connected to many other computers through telephone lines, security becomes even more important. Lieu notes that once a computer is networked, "not only can people pretend they are you, computers can also pretend they are your computers (known as spoofing). . . . On the way from your computer to some other computer, anyone can use a sniffer program to tap in and listen to what you are saying."

So what can be done? Either disconnect your computer—probably not a good idea for most students and businesspeople—or use a "gateway" computer. A gateway is a single computer through which the network is connected to the "outside." This computer should be made as secure as possible, and it should be monitored. It's important to keep logs of who uses a gateway computer and when they use it, to show a pattern of normal usage. Logs may be the only way of tracking an intruder if security is breached. And the rest of the computers in the internal network can be protected by a "firewall"—a software program to protect them from infiltrations.

Those of us who don't have business computer networks still face some important security issues. For example, the original World Wide Web was perfectly safe for computer users until the advent of new applications such as Javascript and ActiveX. Now, just logging onto some websites may allow dangerous code to enter your computer. It's important to run antivirus tests and to download only from those sites that you trust. You should pick unusual passwords and change them frequently. And of course, you should never send personal information, such as passwords, over the Internet or through E-mail without some form of protection.

If your computer is very valuable to your home or business, you should spend sufficient time making it secure. Do you use it to run your home-based business? Then you should calculate how much damage will be done to your business if it is damaged or broken—and then be prepared to spend the time and money required to protect it.

Finally, remember that the number of break-ins that occur is actually very small in comparison to the amount of traffic on the Internet. You can afford to relax a little, once precautions have been taken. As S. M. Lieu notes, "The cracker likewise has a cost-benefit tradeoff. It's unlikely that someone will break into Fort Knox for a box of Wheaties."

Bibliography

Adler, Jerry, and John McCormick. "The DNA Detectives." *Newsweek*, November 16, 1998, 66-71.

Bauman, Adam S. "Internet Hackers Breach Security: Hard-core Porn Stored on Livermore Lab's Computers." *San Jose Mercury News*, July 12, 1997.

"Before They Log On: Teach Your Children Well," *U.S. News and World Report*, January 23, 1995, 60.

Beiser, Vince. "The Cyber-Snoops: How Internet Gumshoes Breach Personal Privacy." *Maclean's*, June 23, 1997.

BloomBecker, Buck. *Spectacular Computer Crimes: What They Are and How They Cost American Business Half a Billion Dollars a Year!* Homewood, Ill.: Dow Jones-Irwin, 1990.

Burroughs, Rich. Http://cause-for-alarm.com/flash/mitnick.html

Caryl, Christian. "Reach Out and Rob Someone: Russia's Hackers." *U.S. News and World Report*, April 21, 1997.

Cavazos, Edward, and Gavino Morin. *Cyberspace and the Law: Your Rights and Duties in the On-Line World.* Cambridge, Mass.: The MIT Press, 1994.

"Child Porn Ring Using America Online Busted," from newsbytes@clarinet.com, September 14, 1995. (See also http://www-swiss.ai.mit.edu/6805/a...rime/FBI-AOL-Newsbytes-9-14-95.txt.)

Computer Crime Investigations Center, http://www.ovnet.com/~dckinder/frmain01.html

Computer Fraud and Abuse Statute of 1986.
Http://www.cpsr.org/cpsr/privacy/crime/fraud.act.txt.

Corley, Eric. "Free the Hacker Two." *Harper's Magazine*, September 1989, 22-25.

"Corporate Security: Forget the Hackers, Bar the Door." *U.S. News and World Report*, May 12, 1997.

"Cyber-Terrorism." *Maclean's*, April 21, 1997.

Denning, Dorothy. "Concerning Hackers Who Break into Computer Systems," 1990.
Http://www.cpsr.org/cpsr/privacy/crime/denning.html

"Drop the Phone: Busting a Computer Whiz." *Time*, January 9, 1989.

Federal Bureau of Investigation National Computer Crime Squad.
Http://www.fbi.gov, E-mail nccs@fbi.gov.

Flock, Jeff. "Surfin' the Net to Track Down Criminals." CNN Interactive, April 23, 1996.
http://cnn.com/TECH/9604/23/internet.crime/index.html

Freedman, David, and Charles Mann. "Cracker: This Computer Geek Could Have Taken Down the Networks of Military Sites, Nuclear-Weapons Labs, Fortune 100 Companies and Scores of Other Institutions." *U.S. News and World Report*, June 2, 1997.

Funk, John. "2 Men, 3 Teens Arrested for Computer Tampering," *Cleveland Plain Dealer*, August 19, 1994.

Gaudin, Sharon. "Security Flaws Force Microsoft to Get Active." *Computerworld*, February 24, 1997.

Gegax, Trent. "Stick 'em up? Not Anymore—Now It's Crime by Keyboard." *Newsweek*, July 21, 1997.

Gill, Mark Stuart. "Cybercops Take a Byte Out of Computer Crime." *Smithsonian*, May 1997.

Gornstein, Leslie. "In Hacking, for Some, the Punishment May Not Fit the Crime." *Fort Worth (Texas) Star-Telegram*, August 19, 1994.

Guyan, Claire. "Computers Give Pupils Access to Bomb Recipes." *Sunday Star-Times* [Wellington, New Zealand], March 27, 1994.

"Hackers Break into America Online," from newsbytes@clarinet.com, September 11, 1995.

Hafner, Katie. "Morris Code." *New Republic*, February 19, 1990.

Hafner, Katie, and John Markoff. *Cyberpunk: Outlaws and Hackers on the Computer Frontier*. New York: Simon and Schuster, 1991.

Haworth, Carla. "Publishers Press Colleges to Stop Software Piracy by Their Students." *Chronicle of Higher Education*, July 11, 1997.

Judson, Karen. *Computer Crime: Phreaks, Spies, and Salami Slicers*. Hillside, N.J., and Hants, U.K.: Enslow Publishers, 1994.

Kapor, Mitchell. "A Little Perspective, Please." *Forbes*, June 21, 1993.

Kerstetter, Jim. "Senate Probes Cyber-Terrorism." *PCWeek*, June 24, 1996.

Labaton, Steven. "Computer Stings Gain Favor as Arrests for Smut Increase." *New York Times*, September 16, 1995.

Laqueur, Walter. "Terrorism via the Internet." *The Futurist*, March/April 1997.

The Law Office Consumer Guide, http://www.thelawoffice.com

Levins, Hoag. "Hackers Devastate Texas Newspaper's Servers." *Editor and Publisher*, June 28, 1997.

Lewin, Tamar. "College Settles Harassment Charges Stemming from Computer Conferences." *New York Times*, September 21, 1994.

Lewis, Peter H. "Company Says Electronic Mail Was Opened to Find Pornography." *New York Times*, September 15, 1995.

———. "Computers Beware! New Type of Virus Is Loose on the Net." *New York Times*, September 4, 1995.

Lopez, Claude-Anne. "Prophet and Loss: Benjamin Franklin, the Jews, and Cyber-Bigotry." *New Republic*, January 27, 1997.

Machlis, Sharon. "Phone Hackers Dial up Trouble." *Computerworld*, February 24, 1997.

McNamara, Connie. "Tracking the Cyberspace Predator." *Reader's Digest*, November 1995, 107-112.

Meyer, Michael. "The Feds in Cyberspace." *Newsweek*, September 25, 1995.

———. "Is This Hacker Evil or Merely Misunderstood?" *Newsweek*, December 4, 1995.

Michals, Debra. "Cyber-Rape: How Virtual Is It?" *Ms.*, March/April 1997.

Mungo, Paul, and Bryan Clough. *Approaching Zero: The Extraordinary*

World of Hackers, Phreakers, Virus Writers, and Keyboard Criminals. New York: Random House, 1992.

National White Collar Crime Center Factsheet, November 1995. Http://www.aspensys.aspensys.com/whcollar.txt.

"Next: Cyberlaundering?" *Economist*, July 26, 1997.

Pappas, Charles. "To Surf and Protect: You Can Stay Private Online, but It'll Cost You." content/mag/9712/pappas9712.html

"The Perils of Buying on the Buzz." *U.S. News and World Report*, December 9, 1996.

Popkin, James, and John Simons. "Natural Born Predators." *U.S. News and World Report*, September 19, 1994.

Rao, Srikumar. "Robocop." *Forbes*, July 7, 1997.

Sandberg, Jared. "Accidental Hacker Exposes Internet's Fragility." *Wall Street Journal*, July 11, 1997.

Scheier, Robert. "Lock the Damned Door!" *Computerworld*, February 10, 1997.

Schwartz, John. "Blame Society, Not the Net, for the Evils Lurking Online." *Washington Post*, November 18, 1996.

Simons, John. "Seeking Victims in Cyberspace." *U.S. News and World Report*, September 19, 1994.

Slatalla, Michelle, and Joshua Quittner. *Masters of Deception: The Gang That Ruled Cyberspace.* New York: HarperCollins, 1995.

Sterling, Bruce. *The Hacker Crackdown: Law and Disorder on the Electronic Frontier.* New York: Bantam Books, 1992.

Sussman, Vic. "Policing Cyberspace." *U.S. News and World Report*, January 23, 1995.

Viles, Peter. "Hackers Plead Guilty in Contest Fraud." *Broadcasting and Cable*, May 3, 1993.

Wallace, Jonathan, and Mark Mangan. *Sex, Laws and Cyberspace*. New York: M & T Books, 1996.

Wanat, Thomas. "Student Charged with Transmitting Child Pornography." *Chronicle of Higher Education*, May 24, 1996.

————. "Two Internet-Savvy Students Help Track Down Hacker." *Chronicle of Higher Education*, March 1997.

Whitelaw, Kevin. "Fear and Dread in Cyberspace." *U.S. News and World Report*, November 4, 1996.

Wilson, David L. "Rice U Repels Hacker Attack." *Chronicle of Higher Education*, February 9, 1994.

————. "Wiesenthal Center Urges Northwestern to Bar Web Page Denying Holocaust." *Chronicle of Higher Education*, May 24, 1996.

————. "Vulnerable Computer Systems." *Chronicle of Higher Education*, May 24, 1996.

Wold, Geoffrey, and Robert Shriver. *Computer Crime, Techniques, Prevention*. Rolling Meadows, Ill.: Bankers Publishing Co., 1989.

Young, Jeffrey R. " 'Indecency' Law Could Have Chilling Effect on Literary and Artistic Works." *Chronicle of Higher Education*, May 24, 1996.

Index

Index

Index

Picture Credits

GINA DE ANGELIS holds a bachelor of arts degree in theater and a master of arts in history. The author of several books for Chelsea House, she lives in Williamsburg, Virginia.

AUSTIN SARAT is William Nelson Cromwell Professor of Jurisprudence and Political Science at Amherst College, where he also chairs the Department of Law, Jurisprudence and Social Thought. Professor Sarat is the author or editor of 23 books and numerous scholarly articles. Among his books are *Law's Violence*, *Sitting in Judgment: Sentencing the White Collar Criminal*, and *Justice and Injustice in Law and Legal Theory*. He has received many academic awards and held several prestigious fellowships. He is President of the Law & Society Association and Chair of the Working Group on Law, Culture and the Humanities. In addition, he is a nationally recognized teacher and educator whose teaching has been featured in the *New York Times*, on the *Today* show, and on National Public Radio's *Fresh Air*.